What Is Home if Not a Person?

by Lindsey Heatherly

Copyright 2022 by Lindsey Heatherly

First published in the United States in 2022 by Skyway Journal

ISBN 978-1-7335280-2-3

ISSN 2766-0141

All rights reserved. No part of this book may be produced in any form or by any electronic or mechanical means, including information storage and retrieval systems, without permission in writing from the publisher, except by a reviewer who may use brief quotations for a book review.

Skyway Journal
Tampa, FL USA

www.skywayjournal.wordpress.com

Twitter: @SkywayJournal

The characters and events in this book are fictitious. Any similarity to real persons, living or dead, is coincidental and not intended by the author.

Cover design by Carrie at Cheeky Covers

For Rylee

Introduction

What's bred in the bone comes out in the flesh.

What frustrates the sleep, what nettles the mind engenders the thought.

What sticks in the craw, what fuddles the tongue, what renders one mute must birth on the page.

Torrent or trickle, the words must come. Piece by piece, word by word, we build a sentence, on page or screen, and shape it and mold it until it approximates what we think we thought. Usually it is not quite the thing, as a sentence can only be the ghost of a thought. Then we surpise ourselves with the realization that maybe this sentence is what we really meant after all. Self-delusion, maybe. Certainly there is a psychological process at work that allows us to accept this bald statement as our own thought. My old English teacher was fond of saying that you don't really know what you think until you write it down.

Twofold result: certain agitations of the psyche can only be fully expressed via the written word, and the very act of writing becomes a release, a parole from the prison of compulsion. If we could articulate with utterance the inner turmoil, who among us would be writers? Not me, and I suspect, not many of you. Inchoate thoughts and the compulsion to sort them out are two of the distinguishing traits of the writer.

Not all we manufacture in our heads emerges muddled and incoherent. It is a relatively simple task to recount a narrative. This happened, then this happened. Also simple is describing the world as it is. And by simple, I do not mean necessarily easy. Thomas Mann observed that a writer is a person for whom writing is more difficult than others. We work at it and by paying attention we can capture the details that ensure the reader believes we're describing the real world. Simple, yes, but it requires talent to craft a driving narrative that hooks the reader, interspersed with the telling details that dispel a reader's disbelief. Claritas & veritas, remain the two essentials drawn from toolbox of the nonfiction writer.

It was as a nonfiction writer that Lindsey Heatherly first came to my attention. She had submitted to Red Fez Magazine a short memoir piece, "Lindsey Waterfall" which the editors adored and this was followed by another, "The Shell with the Hole in the Top". Both were well-structured and insightful narratives that kept the reader engaged. Weeks, months later, I would still think about these two pieces. They had become part of my interior funiture.

For poetry, we oft delve in the deeper places of our psyche. We choose subjects that we may have difficulty addressing directly. We write around the subject, we use figurative language. Lindsey Heatherly submitted "Purple Wisteria" for the Red Fez Poetry Contest in which the theme was "hope". And it was about so much more than just hope. The scene reached out and touched so many threads in the context of a life, and all these threads were intricately woven into an elegant piece, nineteen lines long and yet one beautifully crafted sentence.

Recently we received "Stillness of a Songbird" from Lindsey Heatherly. Like moon poems, I imagine every poet has a dead bird poem in their inventory and yet this piece transcended the banal and commonplace, and actually gave us a moment of grace. I may be biased but I consider these two poems I published in Red Fez Magazine to be among the strongest pieces presented here.

In this collection we get such a variety of easily accessible poems, a panoply of moods and modes in which we see the poet joyous, sad, despairing ,confused, vexed, lonely, frisky, larky, stroppy, thoughtful, abashed, bemused, leery, insouciant, chuffed, chagrined, goofy, timid, outraged, wracked, frazzled, beleaguered, resigned, frivolous, and need I go on? Each poem gives us a glimpse of what it may be like to be inside her skin. We are never more naked than when we write. She is Eve minus the fig leaves.

Claritas. Veritas.

Literature shows us the depth and range of the human condition, and in this small collection, with clarity and honesty, Lindsey

Heatherly calls herself out, caught in the act of being human.

~ Doc Sigerson, RED FEZ Magazine

Praise for What Is Home If Not A Person

Every single poem in *What is home if not a person?* is a revelation. In Lindsey's heart-full work, even the smallest detail is noticed, appreciated, given its due. These poems grapple with the places we once inhabited and the places we'd like to go, geographical and religious roots, longing and hurting and the relentless search (and hope) for something more. This book posits that beauty can be found past the pain, that meaning can be made from all that once tried to crush us. This is a life-affirming, brilliant piece of soul work from Lindsey Heatherly."

- Liza Olson, author of *Here's Waldo*, *The Brother We Share*, and *Afterglow*, EIC of *(mac)ro(mic)*

This achingly honest and tender collection is a precious gift from an artist whose rawness and vulnerability are embedded in every poem, every carefully chosen word. We are granted a glimpse into the life of a mother and daughter as she navigates the types of obstacles and setbacks we can all relate to. She teaches us what it means to love, her poems grabbing us by the collar and shouting, "Do not give up on love, especially the love we hold for ourselves."

-Susan Triemert, author of Guess What's Different

Lindsey Heatherly's collection captures the fragile magic of nature, the rawness of everyday life and the realities of family life, motherhood and relationships. Heatherly writes masterfully with a delicate quality and sharp wit; hope is a tender undertone and despair a brutal reflection - her openness in these beautifully striking pieces pull us into memories, home, and heart; the deep roots of humanity, the reasons why we hurt and why we keep holding on.

Louise Mather, author of The Dredging of Rituals and editor of Acropolis Journal

All at Once	16
A Poem for Our Future	17
A Customer Asks When I Am Due and All I Can Say Is *I'm Not*	19
Darling	21
God Himself Said It Was Okay	22
Waiting In The Car Line at Ten-Till-Nine and the Day Has Faded To Night	24
Psychedelia	25
The Neighbor	27
Untethered	29
I Find A Set of Photos From the Beach	31
A Mercy of Good Things	32
When I Could Not Bear Another Day	33
Funny How	35
There Is a Penny Under My Tongue	38
The Day Before Father's Day	40

I Wonder if You Remember   41

I'm Watching A Star Is Born After Two Glasses
of Chardonnay   42

When I Die   43

Fuck Florida   44

When In Crisis, I Drive to the Dollar General in
Search For Something   45

Nights Like This   46

To Dust You Will Return   47

Stillness of a Songbird   49

Eau De Parfum   51

The Night I Met God In The Drugstore   53

Small Town, Small World   55

When I'm Unsure If I Believe In Fate   57

Taking Out The Garbage on a Sunday Night 59

It's Been Six Years Since I've Lived With a
Significant Other, And I No Longer Remember
What It's Like To Rinse Dishes While Someone

Else Washes   61

When It's My Third Night Of No Sleep, I Dream
I've Gone Insane   63

Mania   65

Outpatient Pharmacy   67

Laundry Day   68

You Want To Be A Better Writer, You Say   69

I Want To Inhale What I Do Not Know   72

After Picking You Up From The House I Grew Up In 74

Spare Room   75

Mushroom Poem   77

Preservation   80

the boys   81

An Egg or Two   83

Stream of Madness   85

Standby   87

Dinner is Served	89
What Am I Waiting For?	91
Saturn	92
Purple Wisteria	94
Be Free, Little Bird	96
Agree to Disagree	98
Honey for Houseflies	101
Eckerd Pharmacy, 2005	103
Highway 25	105
actias luna	107
A Moon Poem	108
Roots Of Our Marrow	110
It is May and I Am Still Waiting	111
Last Night Mom and Dad Bought Dinner From the Local Mexican Restaurant	113
Kaleidoscope	116

Just Enough	117
Chandelier Made of Spoons	118
Eternity	120
I Know I Am Unwell When I Wander Aimlessly Around the Dollar General on a Saturday Night	121
When That Final Day Comes	123
Hot Mustard	124
I Did Ten Minutes and Twenty-One Seconds on the Exercise Bike	125
The Thing That Terrifies Me Most	127
What Is More Beautiful Than This?	128
Acknowledgements	130
About the Author	133

All at Once

I gaze out the window, unmade covers sprawled over the bed as if tussled during a passionate love affair, afternoon light illuminating the room with overcast greys, and I am invited to crawl back in, to lift my one foot still glued to the floor, but I am filled with the buzz of unfinished tasks abandoned during the hour I used to take a shower and rub lotion over my worn, tired body, massaging gentle circles over dry skin, devoting care and attention to each nail, cutting away months of dead skin around each cuticle during an hour that could have been used to fold towels, wash dishes, run the washer, clean the bathroom, take out the trash, and I notice the maintenance man's Jeep parked nearest the office, the building I can see directly from my bedroom window, and I watch how he moves with restraint, how urgency knows not his name—the click of his cowboy boots on pavement provide a tempo perhaps the plants enjoy, a sound I cannot make with clipped fingernails. I notice the grass and clovers, overgrown, and wonder if they love the click-clack noise—how they grow with wild abandon!—slowly, then all at once, and I wonder if I am growing slowly now.

A Poem for Our Future

I look through old photos and find one of you

crouched in the laundry basket watching television

in the living room, cramped between the recliner

and oversized bean bag chair. I remember

how constricted we were in that apartment,

how you always wanted your own bathroom,

how I used to tell my mother the same.

How we fought and cried, laughed and made up,

until the walls shook with conviction.

We lived.

We lived every tired, exhilarating, mundane,

irritating, calm, comforting moment to the absolute

best of our abilities.

The walls knew it.

The wind chime hanging from the balcony knew it.

The worn carpet and cracked tile knew it.

Each small joy, each glaring imperfection,

a breadcrumb leading us Here.

You. Me.

It was a privilege, those days.

And even now when you look at me like you do.

In passing, I see.

A Customer Asks When I Am Due And All I Can Say Is *I'm Not*

the sounds of the pharmacy hush

as if I am underwater—not drowning, no, observing

the person with a face like mine standing there

behind the register, too stunned to disclose

that stress has given her a period and bloated stomach

for four weeks straight, she can no longer

ignore the dark circles under her eyes

when she brushes her teeth before bed,

the gray hairs that sprout through

the middle of her latte-colored eyebrows

are nearly impossible to cover,

when she crafts a poem she must do so quickly

between tasks, otherwise

they might not exist, and her body,

this vessel for a soul, a weary soul, feels

so completely washed up, used up, discarded,

worse for wear, and the customer bows her head

as if in prayer, eyes averted, as paper waves

of bags and receipts crash into her abdomen,

and I watch the person with a face like mine

come up for air, soaking wet.

<u>Darling</u>

Do not despair. Even with your gaze
cast down, beautiful things can be found

at your feet. On my walk I found a cubic
zirconia pendant and a golden dragonfly

with wings veiled in morning light—a weed
that looked like a succulent thriving

between the cracks of concrete on the gravel
walking track—I watched a white feather

float down, down, down, and a piece of trash
that looked like a seahorse that whispered

keep going, keep going, keep going.

God Himself Said It Was Okay

that I could let go—in the most dismissive voice
ever to exist.

If God were a fraternity brother. If I were a
crumpled can

of beer the morning after. Hundreds of us
around.

Used up. Discarded. Add to the pile

in the trash bag on the corner of the porch.

You can let go, he said to his friend

in the khaki shorts and Rainbow flip-flops.

I'm sorry, I thought you were talking to me.

Aluminum tumbles down swollen oak steps

past the water hose, the marigolds—

closer to death than I thought I was—next

to the fake rock with a spare key:

knock, knock. *Hello, can you hear me?*

But there is no string attached to this can.

Waiting In The Car Line At Ten-Till-Nine And The Day Has Faded To Night

I can hear the band music, the xylophone, wafting out into the crisp fall night, tears streaming down my cheeks, my hair in a bun on top of my head, my clothes mismatched. I have not showered but bathed in immense sadness, and I wonder why my favorite time of year is also the time I fall deep into that dark pull, edging closer to what I am scared of, what I try most not to become, and then I see her silhouette and I know—it will be okay because it has to be. There is no other option.

Psychedelia

I watched him bend at the knees

his six-foot-six frame a praying mantis

that tightened into a paper crane

& collapsed into streams of confetti as I followed

him out that rooftop window. The sky

was a backdrop of purple-orange ribbons

& electricity towers glowed fire

between the pines on the mountaintop ahead.

His bare foot tapped loose shingles

as psychedelia played from his busted-up phone

& I traced the home-drawn circles

that danced on his legs. He looked through the trees

into the horizon & saw California—

told stories to anyone who would listen

stories of a simpler life, one lived on a commune

& how he once clipped buds for twenty bucks an hour

& he left, *Oh, why did I leave?*

He took a drag from his last Marlboro Red

& gazed out into the Carolina sunset. I reached

for his hand. *I'd give anything to go back*

he said & his hand became a moth

with fractal wings that fluttered on his cheek.

The Neighbor

The tiny dog yaps from the second-floor balcony with each lap.

Having lost count on, let's say, lap number six, I notice a glow

from the shadow seated behind the ankle-biter. *Hey, Lindsey*,

the shadow says, and I cannot remember her name. Jessica or Jennifer?

Maybe. *Hey, how are you?* Pleasantries count for something, I think.

Sixteen years since high school, and I cannot remember her name.

She handed me coffee through the drive thru one morning and addressed

me by name. Sometimes I think my brain survives by forgetting.

Picking and choosing are not for beggars. Take them all. The memories.

I am rich with abandonment. I wonder how one remembers. Maybe I will check the yearbook. Maybe next time I will remember.

Untethered

A balloon floats towards space—

only it never pops.

It stays the same, filled

with the closet's musty air

where old letters and the bracelet

you once bought me rests

in the top drawer of the jewelry box I found

that one time at the thrift store down the road

from the pawn shop, that time

you cleared it out and sold

my grandmother's necklace for

less than a tank of gas.

Why do the things that ground me disappear?

I have this scarf here—

I feel it like the ring I kept from view.

I circle it round and round my pinkie.

It rests in the same spot.

I wonder if the stars ever lose their grip,

look down at us through musty air

and call it hope.

I Find A Set Of Photos From The Beach

The sand is grey with a gentle salt lamp glow.

There is a tree, and the sun has set perfectly

between the branches. Ripples in the ocean

form a maze to nirvana. The woman is glowing.

I do not know her name. In that moment, I know

peace exists. I save the photo, keep it for myself.

That is the answer. To the fog. To desire, to hope.

The inner dialogue when they are too quiet.

They want a woman who is not me. So I will take

myself for who I am. I will hold myself. No more

waiting. No more wondering. You cannot twist

the branches of the tree to hold the sun.

A Mercy of Good Things

When a string of unexpectedly good things

settle onto my lap, I wonder if God has chosen

to give me a life full of goodness to take the place

of an eternity meant only for those who have not denied

their father in heaven. I remember asking my dad,

when I was young, and he was still a preacher,

how so many bad people have such wonderful lives,

and he told me sometimes God provides a mercy

to those whose end will be in the pit of fire, and I'm left

to wonder if I broke the last straw and the good

happening in my life is a mercy afforded me

by a god who gave up.

When I Could Not Bear Another Day

I slept. Told my daughter I loved her as she left

for school, and I slept for three more hours. In a day,

perhaps we all need more time. When seconds

are too strenuous to fill, I watch them go by. I lie down

in the sheets that are a tad too small for the mattress

and open my eyes, vision blurry, watch the sun

leave angels on the wall. I take a photo to keep the angel

close. My guardian. She is gone now.

I see her in the slivers of gold in the spider web

outside my window. It glistens and gleams a promise

that there is beauty in what is fragile. Even hope.

How quickly it leaves, like the angel. It sways in the wind, knowing it could vanish at any moment. It always comes

back, though. The web. The garden spider always rebuilds,

even if in a different place. I wonder how many times hope

has returned. I wonder what the life span is—

of the spider, of myself, of the butter I melted in the pan

to fry two eggs. There is something calm in watching

what is natural. Butter melts, spider webs break, angels

appear when we least expect them. There is a lizard

on the screen of my window. He has a blue tail, yellow

lines that run the length of his body, and I watch one line

flutter like a string—guitar, harp, heart, and I am reminded

good can find us, even when we shut the door.

Funny How

I smashed the box

of granola bars against the kitchen

counter. The box is ruined. The granola is,

most likely, in crumbs. Some things

cannot be returned. There is standing water

in my bathtub. The water has nowhere

to go. The dishwasher is broken. My computer

screen is frozen as I sit down to write. The mouse

spins and it spins and my anger spins—

round and round we go. I am trying

to buy a house. The one I looked at tonight

smelled like death. As the realtor tried to open

the front door, the blinds that hung from the closest

window swung back and forth.

She laughed as we stood in the dark

and said, *Hopefully that's not someone inside.*

Funny how we laugh fear away. My daughter

is mad at me, and I am mad at my daughter,

and I am completely empty. I have nothing left

to give anyone. I am afraid I will die alone.

Haha. Hahahaha. Laugh the fear away. I stare

at the flame in the candle so long

a dark spot floats around the room.

Sometimes I am so full

of hatred that even the ones I love most

are not exempt. I am tired of doing it all, always tired

of doing it all, so I raised my voice.

Slammed the door and the dishes into the sink.

Stomped my feet like a toddler. So full.

Funny how rage expands to inhabit *more*.

Funny how much yelling looks like laughing.

Laugh the fear away. I wonder if plants ever get angry.

If the burden of being stuck is ever too much to bear—

this life. The candle flickers. I am waiting

for all these dark spots to clear.

There Is a Penny Under My Tongue

I cannot hold this muscle, this lashed-out grit

turned limp. It tastes of metal and Vienna sausages

straight from the can. Straight down the middle, the heart

of the matter, what matter? Hold your tongue for me,

like mine and pinch the penny between your thumb and forefinger.

Spin it on the kitchen table between

the neighbor's dog and my grandmother's dead cat.

Heads, cut your losses. Tails, well, the sky is incapable of such

untruths. Does the violet sky lose when the sun dips underwater, taking

all light with it? I wonder if pennies absorb the light

they reflect. If they fish strings of it from boiling water

to toss at the refrigerator door, see what sticks. The sun hides

in my pocket while the violet sky wonders if it should have been a bird.

Or a fish. Something with wings, fins, some way to direct

the falling stars upwards, back into the sky, away

from the gravel crunching under my feet.

The Day Before Father's Day

We say we are happy alone

the same way we tell strangers at dollar stores

that strawberry-flavored drink mix

is better than cherry.

We mean it, but lightly.

I almost said I love you.

You said those feelings were gone.

Strawberry is better than cherry.

I drink my water plain.

I forgive you.

I Wonder if You Remember

I think about that holiday movie where the girl is on a date and rushes to get home because she accidentally took laxatives instead of antacids, and how he rips her corset off just as she gets into the bathroom, and how he washes her off in the shower and lies next to her in bed and promises he won't ever tell anyone about how she shit her pants on Halloween night, and I think about the time you quietly discarded my soiled pants in the garbage outdoors after I shit my pants while we were on vacation at the beach and how you cleaned the bathroom and swore you'd never tell anyone, and I wonder if you tell her my embarrassing stories, like that one, and you both cackle over my humanness, or worse, if you never think of it at all. I wonder if you remember it, remember protecting me, guarding me, caring for me, in the ways you knew how before destroying me completely, all at once, in a million separate ways.

I'm Watching A Star Is Born After Two Glasses Of Chardonnay

an hour after my daughter comes home from her eighth-grade dance and I keep asking myself, *What do I want more than anything in the world?* What would bring me the most joy? I wish I could sing in front of a huge audience and perform perfectly as myself and be received by thousands of people, but I am an introvert. I know this is not what I am capable of. What I want more than anything is to be exactly myself and to be loved for it. For one person to look me in the eyes when I'm depressed, when I'm enthusiastic, when I'm angry, take my hand in theirs and say, *Yes, this is what I want.* I finish my wine and watch the scene where Lady Gaga performs on stage for the first time with Bradley Cooper. I truly believe whatever is meant to happen, will. I will never sing to a packed stadium. I may never find the kind of love we all long for. But I hope to one day express myself wholly and authentically with my words, if simple and absolute. I do not watch the movie to the end.

When I Die

let me come back as a waterfall

Fuck Florida

I picture you leaning back in the lawn chair with a Coke can in your left hand, your laughter catching in foggy breaths wafting into the winter night. The yellow glow from the kitchen window shines onto the deck, onto your face, and you look like a burly angel with auburn hair. Your plaid shirt and blue jeans, the watch your wife bought you for Christmas, the hat mom and dad bought you the year your team finally won, and you ran circles around the house we grew up in yelling at the top of your lungs. You ask me if I'm okay and I choke back tears because I know you're the only one who gets me, truly gets me, and I wonder who will get me when you're gone. You're already so far away.

When In Crisis, I Drive To The Dollar General In Search Of Something

other than water but the stocker stops me before I can reach the rows of carbonated water in the back, tells me how hours are cut and she cannot help everyone, and they cannot keep everything in stock, and she cannot run the front of the store and stock the shelves, she is only one person, and a part of me withers because I remember this, only now it is worse, much worse. I buy citrus tea that I will not drink because of the sugar content. I vowed to quit soda after my dentist shaved my tooth down for a crown, and I realize this is no better. I do not restrict these things because I am trying to be healthy. As if health were that easy to control. As if my teeth would not crack from the weight of my thoughts. I cut them because I do not want things to get worse. I am always bracing for the next broken tooth. I come home and light the warm vanilla sugar candle so I can feel some warmth, some relief, some comfort, and the reflection of the flame flickering in the window catches my attention. I clench my jaw and turn to make sure the bookcase is not on fire.

Nights Like This

I feel your arms reach round my waist to embrace me, and I feel the vibrato of your voice on my neck. The gentle purr of your laugh soothes me, if only for a moment, until I am snapped back to the reality of *now*, and my stomach turns sour. Which is worse: to buckle at the knees on an autumn Wednesday or to believe that you once loved me?

To Dust You Will Return

Did you know you can go for a walk without changing your clothes? You can go in what you're wearing? It's okay if there is no time for one whole hour of fast paced walking squeezed in before the day is up? You don't have to change into a sports bra, work out pants, t-shirt, running shoes?

I went for a short walk tonight wearing the scrubs I wore to work. The wind was blowing with purpose, reflection.

So mysterious, the moon. Not one photo I took turned out, but I can tell you it was a moment I will remember. Me, standing there, in the field next to the armory-turned-gym with a lonesome flagpole to my right, the moon, yellow and warm, suspended in the branches of the trees, clouds sprawled out in the harshest of lines, lines straighter than I could ever make with a ruler spanning the length of the horizon in front of me, wires cutting through time itself. I wanted to sit right there. I was afraid if I did I would never return.

To feel alive, like that. It's no wonder we drown it out with life.

A funny thing it is, to have breath in your lungs and still forget to breathe. Take the long way home. Say hi to the cows. Come as you are. Run your hands through the dirt. Do you feel it? Spend an extra moment with the stars. To dust you will return.

Stillness Of A Songbird

His wings were quiet, blue, brilliantly pinned

to springtime asphalt between the railroad tracks and VFW,

nestled among the pines and discarded takeout containers,

beside a crumpled pair of child-size blue jeans

and a box of cardboard merlot.

I am reminded the ground knows no difference

between the blossoms that fall from the tulip tree and my hands—

the softness that cradled and laid his feathers to rest

underneath a single black tupelo leaf.

I hear the trill of the screech-owl and wonder if she knows

what it is to be grounded—surely, she does not!

What a strange thought: to ask a river if it knows stillness.

I ask the sky if the clouds know their bounds,

if glory can be found within restraint, and I wring

my hands, again, willing my rough edges smooth.

Eau De Parfum

I remember when she once changed her clothes in front of me. Her breasts were large and hung halfway down her waist to rest on her soft, rounded belly. Bottles of perfume lined her white vanity, the one that I painted in the backyard as a teenager, used in my bedroom, and now sits in the home I grew up in. I would try each one—each spray a tally mark on my arm, an indication of how grown I would become one day. Her jewelry box was overflowing with rings and necklaces, and her engagement ring was a gift reserved for my eighteenth birthday. I wonder what it would be like to talk to her now. If she would pull me into her arms, embrace me, clutch me towards her chest, or if she would quickly pat me on the head and assure me it will all be fine as she fastens her bra and digs through her closet, like my sister, like myself, searching for a different dress, a different love, acceptance. I wonder if we are alike. I wonder, if she were alive now, if I could tell her the things I keep from everyone else. I wonder if she would understand, if she would stop cleaning the kitchen, baking the cornbread, talking on the phone, and tapping the ashes of her cigarette into the ashtray. If she would take me by the shoulders, look me in the eyes, and assure me that I am a woman from a line of fighters and not from a line of hysterical women. That I've been through hell, and she has too, but we are strong, and our daughters need us to lead them. I wonder if she would tell me the road is lonely, desolate, but that she and my ancestors are proud of the woman I have become. That I have carried on their legacy, and I am resilient. That I will not end my life.

The Night I Met God In The Drugstore

I met God

in the aisle between

analgesics and wound care.

I was no longer in search

for healing, so I settled

for superficial repairs.

He offered to cleanse me,

to save me from myself,

so He took a box of Band-Aids,

peeled each one apart,

and placed them across His skin.

He said, *I am the body*,

and I asked if He would remember me.

Hush, child, He whispered,

as His index finger brushed

my cheek and landed upon my lips.

Healing is given to those

who want to be saved.

Small Town, Small World

crank the car and turn   the heat on high.

      smell dog shit. check   the bottom of each shoe.

clear. maybe   it's the defroster. or the heat.

put the car   in reverse and block   the sun

from your eyes. you want   to feel comforted, so point

the car in the direction   of your favorite bookstore. change

your mind   two miles in and change course
      to the *tobacco shop*—

you like their crystals and incense. you don't
      know

how crystals work or if   they work but
you like how   they feel

in your palms. speed   past the turn and take a
left   at the light.

you don't feel   like inhaling incense
smoke and don't   care

to hold anything in your hands but   maybe
      you'll cook

something, so point   your car towards the grocery store. stop

at the red light and notice   people gathering on the street

in camping chairs and on truck beds and realize

it is winter   and Christmastime which means *parade* and   *of course*

they'll have a parade on this small street,
    in this small town,

small world. make   a left at the grocery store on your   right

and turn around   in the gas station, otherwise   you'll be stuck

for an hour and there is   nothing you want   to eat

badly enough to sit   and wait   in that small parking lot,

small town, small world. point   your car towards   home

and think about how there is   nothing
    you want

other than to want   something.

When I'm Unsure If I Believe In Fate

I think of that night I wandered alone downtown

and stumbled across the bookstore my sister spoke of—

the one with the chandelier made of spoons—

and I browsed hundreds of books and found little collections of poetry

and thought what an idea it was to have such powerful words

condensed into something to be read in one sitting.

I picked one that spoke of wild hair and thought of

the curls I force straight and my personality, and how it would be nice

to let go and be free, so I flipped through the pages and

spent the last bit of cash I had to cradle hope within my hands.

How four years later I am sitting here with my laptop

drafting a poem about you and downtown and cobblestones

when I feel the sudden urge to hold that book in my hands.

I scour it from my collection, flip a few pages in, and realize

the publisher is the same one that recently accepted a story of mine.

I am comforted to know that I am exactly where I need to be,

writing what I need to write, and that is the greatest gift of all.

Taking Out The Garbage On A Sunday Night

Frogs bellow
their grievances
and crickets chirp
their dues.
My shirt hangs
from my shoulder,
less elegant
than the spider
building his web,
rising and falling
in the shadows
nearest the rain gutter
that leads
to the sidewalk
where I carry
the trash to prepare
for the new week.
Two flashes catch
my eye as I approach
the dumpster,
and I pause.
She stands her ground
and I nod my head,
accepting her territory.
For feral cannot
exist without fear.
White whiskers
catch moonlight
and black fur blends

into asphalt.
I toss the garbage,
walk back and wonder
if frogs and crickets
fear things
they cannot know
and if cats ever long
to sing their songs
to the dark.

It's Been Six Years Since I've Lived With A Significant Other And I No Longer Remember What It's Like To Rinse Dishes While Someone Else Washes

Do people share chores anymore?

I could scrub the toilet if you wipe down the tub. And I will vacuum

if you put the clothes in the dryer and start another load. We could fold

clothes together as we watch tv. You can pick. I don't care

what we watch, as long as I'm with you. I'd even watch golf.

And I hate golf.

We could cook dinner together. I can chop the onions and potatoes

if you'll prepare the ribs. When you pass behind me to reach

for the spices, you can say *behind* like on *Chopped* and I'll laugh and you'll smack the back pocket of my blue jeans and peck my cheek.

And then we can eat on the porch and watch the birds and the squirrels

and the sunset and you'll tell me you ate way too much

and I'll just nod and say *boy, it was good, though*

and we'll go for a walk down the dirt road to the creek and listen

to the water and cicadas and I'll nuzzle into your shoulder

and you'll kiss my face and pull my body into yours,

and mid make-out session you'll ask if I'm ready to go home,

with a whisper in my ear, and you'll string me along with your lips

until we close and lock the door and leave the dishes for tomorrow.

When It's My Third Night Of No Sleep, I Dream I've Gone Insane

and that my legs are running

in the same yard I played kickball in when I was seven.

I collapse and dig my fingernails into my skin—

relentless itching that refuses to succumb to my efforts.

I notice another woman, a blonde frail ghost

of a person I do not recognize, mirroring my actions.

I hear Mama calling me home and I watch

the setting sun morph to cast-iron black.

And then I erupt through the front door and

steady myself at the kitchen counter and

wonder how she could possibly be standing.

I ask about her spine, and she says they gave her

three epidurals but none of them worked.

She shrugs and bends to take a blackberry pie

out of the oven, and she looks happy and normal

and her hair is golden like the sun thirty minutes

before sundown, and I am reminded of the text

she sent me the morning everything changed,

how she said one day we would all sit

around the table together – but I knew.

I knew we would never gather,

together or apart, and I mourn.

Mania

Hell, I know I've fucked up

a thousand different times

in a million different ways

and that sometimes holding on

is gripping sheets by the fistful

and packing fabric into the hole in your chest

until it reaches your legs, your feet

your arms, your hands

until your body is the escape route for your mind

tell me what thing I did that broke the grace

appointed me at birth

tell me what it was I did so terribly

for this hell to come round

like clockwork, round and round,

a carousel of tricks, ways to die,

ways to try

to not slip through the cracks

every damn time

Outpatient Pharmacy

I said it was probably this weather

as she yawned and pointed and said,

I love that, gesturing to the dove tattoo

on my ring finger. I told her I got it done

after my divorce, and she paused. A rumble

of laughter broke through her lips,

and she lifted her hand for a high five.

Her son asked what was funny. I can still

hear her laughter echoing down the hall.

Laundry Day

The bottoms of my feet shift

loose linoleum squares after lathering my skin

with dollar store lotion on a Sunday

afternoon. I transfer towels to the dryer,

pulled ten inches from the wall

so the vent can breathe, and I wash

a load of work clothes, enough

for two days, because I cannot bear

to do more than I must. It would be tragic,

this life, if perfection came first.

I release my breath and bend

at the waist to lift a sock from the floor.

The tile sticks to my foot, freeing itself.

You Want To Be A Better Writer, You Say

after reading a new piece in Tahoma Literary

Review. You should buy a copy of this issue, read it

cover to cover. That's an effective way to learn.

It will be an investment. What if something happens

and you need money later this week or next? You should

save the money. But how will you ever get better?

How will your writing improve when you cannot afford

to take workshops or classes? How will your writing improve

when you are exhausted from work and parenting

and surviving? Maybe you're meant to observe.

To *feel,* as if you don't feel enough. Feeling for you

is a drug. Every time you read something that resonates,

that tilts your soul on its axis, you crave more. You must

have it. You say screw it and buy the issue, because right now,

this is living. Right now all you want is to feel something,

and this did it. The issue will be delivered to your home.

You'll carry it inside and it will rest on the kitchen table

until the weekend comes. You will be too exhausted

to do anything other than what is necessary, so you fold

laundry, prepare food, pick up around the apartment, clean

the bathroom, prepare for the week ahead. You will move

the issue to the nightstand where it will sit on top of seven other books. The other pile has eight. You will glance at it

each night. It will be a platform for the contact solution

and face cream. It will hold a menu from the restaurant

you tried two weeks back. It will not move. But you will.

And as you head out for work you will linger,

look back and wonder if your words will ever rest

on someone else's nightstand.

I Want To Inhale What I Do Not Know

let it settle, stain the walls of my lungs

with tobacco-laden permanence

I want to swallow the space *between*

before the void bursts forth from my lips

splatters onto my shirt in tie-dye constellations

that chart a future beyond sailboats and land

so that we're back here

eating pasta and snickerdoodle

cobbler made from dollar store ingredients

that were left in the oven for far too long

where you are young and free

and perfect and happy

and I wonder if cats ponder things

they do not know, and I watch our cat reach

for the ornaments on the tree in the corner

draped in white twinkly lights

that look like hope

After Picking You Up From The House I Grew Up In

I point to the field in passing and say *Look at the baby!* as I catch a glimpse of a young brunette, hair cascading over her shoulders, baby staring, wide-eyed, full of wonder, surrounded by April winds and grass, green as the pacifier in his mouth. You ask me, alarmed, *Where is a baby?* for two days ago I told you about the black spot I noticed on my tooth, how I obsessed over this rot in my mouth, how I checked it in the mirror the next morning and it was gone, vanished, and you lowered your head, your voice, confirmed that you could hear me brushing my teeth over and again, that you wondered what was wrong. I point and say, *Over there!* Still, you do not see the baby. *In the grass!* I say, almost nervous-like, and—is the baby there? thank god—you see it. I laugh, doubled over the steering wheel, convulsions bubbling over into this calm moment: that baby with the green pacifier and its mama, a painting in the field on the drive home.

Spare Room

Show me your trash bags, your duffels,

your backpacks and suitcases.

Show me the things you carry and conceal

across your shoulder, beneath your feet,

inside your throat, under your tongue –

the things no one else can ever know,

should ever know, and I will show you mine.

We can decorate the spare bedroom

with shelves and boxes the colors of your heart

with labels like *grief* and *regret* in gold-laced silver.

We can add a sofa and chair, a floor lamp and rug

and make a life out of combining and organizing.

It will take time, but when time is all we have,

we can never be poor.

We can visit that room when we feel

the pull of our identities and wonder

where we came from, who we will be,

and *if it even matters*.

We will plant our own tree in the backyard

with the seeds of our youth and water them

with the mistakes of our past and together

they will grow the most beautiful fruit, the kind

we will pick from the branches and savor

when the sky turns a brilliant orange

and we welcome, together, the night.

Mushroom Poem

I remember trying to locate the trail once I arrived at the river and how I looked for the white dot spray-painted on a tree, any tree, but couldn't find one. I knew I hadn't driven four hours only to get to this spot, this river, with moss covered trees lining the beds of the forest, with large rocks smoothed by the current, only to turn around and drive home. I knew if I walked down the side of the river, it wouldn't make sense. Would I follow the river to go up a mountain? So, I crossed it. The hiking boots I found at Goodwill for ten bucks weren't exactly waterproof. The wool socks would be wet, but I didn't care. I had to keep moving. It was morning and dark and the trees were still and quiet. But the acorns—I could hear acorns falling. I was alone until I met the Appalachian trail and came across two hikers, men, on their way through. They said hello, both wearing bandanas over their foreheads, one with curls matted to the sweat on his brow. The taller one asked me if I had come across any bears.

No, not yet, I said.

I had only seen a bear once, on the Hike Inn Trail, a trail that would lead to a lodge only accessible by hiking. I remember hearing what I thought was a deer rustling in the woods only to look up and see a brown bear. I remember I kept my head down and walked quietly until I safely passed the animal.

If you hear the acorns falling, it means there's a bear in the trees. They like to climb, said the man with the curls.

I thanked them in passing and tried not to think about the acorns.

There was a particular section of the Appalachian Trail where the everything was dark and foggy. I could see no more than about ten feet ahead of me, but I kept on ahead. I kept going.

When I made it to Mt. Cammerer, I met a man with his dog. A black lab or maybe a golden retriever.

I climbed the boulders to get to the top. A wooden, full circle view in the top of that fire tower.

A butterfly landed on my purple hiking pants.

I signed my name in Sharpie: Lindsey minus the Heatherly plus my father's name.

Ran my fingers along the walls. Looked out—only fog.

Sat and waited. Fog dissipated.

Mountains.

Preservation

I want to take my ungloved hands

and scoop the frost

from the driver's side mirror.

I want to place it on my skin

and watch it melt,

sink into my arm.

I want to taste it,

pack it into my throat,

into my chest

until it reaches my heart

and can preserve

what little warmth I have left

the boys

the sun beats down on my crossed arms

and I watch the kids two rows down

gulp from half-empty Mountain Dew bottles

hot dog backwash sloshing as they cheer

hold their gloved hands up, up for the foul ball

and the men a few seats to the right

who probably have names like Ricky or Hank

and drink beer in place of water blow smoke

from twice lit cigarettes and puffed out chests

like territorial primates that skipped work

and knocked one of the kids onto concrete

to snatch the ball from underneath them

and all I can wonder is *Where are their mommas?*

and feel the urge to jump up and snatch the man

who looks like a Ricky up by his collar but instead

I watch the kid sip from his Mountain Dew
bottle

a moment of silence and Ricky and Hank

are scratching their balls and throwing shit

and I ask myself *Do they even realize it?*

I listen to the folks beside me sing along

to "Sweet Caroline" and watch the boys take

a seat and oh how I hate that song

An Egg Or Two

Sometimes when the world is big and my thoughts

linger I pull the skillet from the cabinet nearest the stove

and add a pat of butter to the pan. I watch it melt and crack

an egg and then another and notice translucence fade

to white while yellow bulbs glisten under heat.

I place my bread in the toaster that once perched

on my grandmother's kitchen counter—

nothing fancy, only practical—

and I wonder if my body is just that, to be used

to prepare the same offerings, served

a hundred silent ways, until I am performing in unison

with each former version of myself that slathered

mayonnaise over honey-wheat bread hoping

to make something new out of these broken shells.

Stream of Madness

I'm exhausted and I'm angry and I hate myself and I want to be known but I hate being judged I need to throw the clothes in the wash I want to quit that project I started I'm tired of expectations I hate my body I hate that I'm fat I want to be skinny and dainty and quiet I don't want to take up space I want to be what men want but I also want to be myself I want to be loved by someone who sticks around I don't want to have to explain myself I don't want to give feedback on that piece tonight but if I wait until tomorrow I might not feel well enough to do it it's another thing to add to the list I want to quit social media I want to quit everything literary I want to skip work tomorrow I want to go on a trip I want to want someone who wants me back I don't want to listen to her talk about her ex and I know I do the same thing sometimes I am such a hypocrite I need to get the oil changed on Saturday I need to eat better food I need to eat less I need to spend less time on Twitter I need to figure out how to find comfort when everything is scratchy wool on my skin I want silence and waterfalls and a black hole and the Aurora Borealis my head hurts I want to cry but I'm too tired the vaccine

comes tomorrow which is good but I dread
people don't like me when I share who I am I'm
not easy to handle or swallow I make things
difficult I want peace I feel like my old life was a
hundred years ago he isn't talking to me why
am I surprised he only wants to talk when he's
horny maybe that's all men I want to die I don't
say that much anymore but it's true sometimes
it would be easier you know? to have all this
behind me I hope the laundry dries by morning

Standby

So, yeah, I lied. I said I didn't need anyone.

That I was used to being alone.

That you didn't need to apologize.

That I wanted truth, not bullshit.

That it felt hopeless but shouldn't matter.

Not in the way that feeling hopeless doesn't matter,

but in the way that the feeling of hopelessness

shouldn't be allowed to penetrate my defenses,

much like passing a dead skunk on the highway

on the morning commute to work—

it doesn't break my heart,

it only causes my nose to crinkle and I nod my head

to recalibrate as I drive on down the road,

taking sips of coffee to cover the scent.

I wonder if you thought I thought I didn't matter.

Because I think I do. Matter. I didn't lie about that.

You apologized but said *it's true*.

The truth. That it's not hopeless.

I said it feels hopeless.

That sometimes I wish I had back up, you know?

I'm still waiting to see if you do.

<u>Dinner is Served</u>

The guy who wore dickies and drove
a Kia Soul paid for a rent-by-the-hour joint
at the Super 8 across from the Cracker Barrel
right off the interstate. Guilty eyes scan
the lobby and gain attention from the front,
dash up the steps, 80's era electric geometric,
and tap, tap, tap on room number 203.
Hold breath in lungs until the click of the lock
swings the door open wide and keep
your gaze down, eyes down, notice
the neon triangles and circles in the squares
of carpet, until you see him in the mirror
and he embraces you like a robe in a Hilton
but this is a Super 8, and you've got an hour
or two, and we all know steak is steak,
whether on a platter or trash can lid,
but even now, you still remember his hands.

What Am I Waiting For

Something to move me

Saturn

I pour leftover eggnog in a repurposed spaghetti jar and walk

to the nearest field. The winter air is electric, and the wind

seems to welcome something new. I find them in the app on my phone,

straight ahead. Saturn and Jupiter blink hello. I raise my glass, nod

my head and follow them back home. The closer I get

the less I can see so I sneak through the dark woods and whisper

my final farewell through the trees. I fill my lungs and feel

the wind cut me in half. Sometimes I wonder if

I will remember these things when I take my last breath. The glow

of the salt lamp reminds me. That pale-yellow hue, golden-hour honey,

bumblebees, eggnog, the softness of light—isn't it something?

Purple Wisteria

When he says *your hair is sexy*

the way the gray strands peek through

I think of red velvet church pews

and my mama's peppermint gum breath

and I hear her whisper *look how young she looks*

into my prepubescent ear as the once yin and yang tousles

that danced above the collar bone of the woman seated

in the pew two rows back were replaced with a brilliant black hue

I think of how *youth* means vibrant and useful and necessary

how it must be kept permanent, unchanging, unlike time

unlike growing children and how they stretch our bodies

and minds become oceans to dive deep if only

my eyebrows are defined so the green in my
eyes pop

like the wisteria that glows purple on a rainy
Carolina day

and I am reminded that gray can enhance curls
and hope

for when I see overcast skies I am reminded of
how

the sun is vibrant and useful and necessary

but would scorch the wisteria

were it not for the clouds

Be Free Little Bird

I clench the warbler in my palm—fringe bursting through tight fingers.

I urge beady eyes to fly but do not soften my grip.

Be free, little bird, be free.

I lift my fist to the sky—a little higher now.

Yellow feathers split wide in strain. Up, up, up I reach.

Be free, little bird, be free.

Furrowed brows grapple for reason as I stomp towards the bushes,

fold to my knees, and shove towards the fountain.

Be free, little bird, be free.

I pry open my ribcage and thrust my fist inside.

I feel my heartbeat in my hand—or is that freedom?

Be free, little bird, be free.

Agree to Disagree

Would God still love and forgive me

if I asked Him to consider agreeing to disagree?

Would He welcome a meeting with me,

taking an unassuming seat across the table—

the same hands that wove the strands of the universe

into being, clasped around a simple cup of coffee—

calmly waiting for me to gather my notes,

diagrams, and extensive research consisting

of numbers, tallied scenarios, and conscious

mistakes displaced by honorable deeds?

Would He observe me in wonder as His creation,

light dancing within the star-filled expanse of His eyes,

allowing me to build and present my defense,

aware that I gave everything—every minute,

every thought, every breath, to prepare to speak in

reverence to the One who holds the world in His hands?

Would He be attentive and patient with my emotions?

Would He listen to me cry, bang my fist out of anger,

or raise my voice in passion, or would He bellow

in reproof, silencing my simple, uneducated,

doubt-filled views, referring me, with indignation,

to the text He breathed life into so long ago?

Honey for Houseflies

You wave the back of your hand
and strap up your jaw

Leave honey out for houseflies
and cover your ears as you pray

You read your biography
and smash the pages into your skin

Maybe the words will stick this time

You cry when you forget
and you know mountains do too

So you collect dandelions
and crush them into your chest

You wait for them to take root

and spread among your desert heart

But there are places even weeds refuse to grow

Eckerd Pharmacy, 2005

I am now the age of the woman

I worked with when I was eighteen.

A worn-out mother who wore a bracelet

with the name *Lindsey* round her wrist.

She drank Diet Pepsi and nestled a bottle

between rows of pharmaceutical grade ice packs

in the freezer every morning around eleven

for a slushy treat by lunchtime.

Her weight was an issue but mine was not,

I thought, not then, and now I am her

and I too have felt the pain of loss and rebirth

and wonder about her and her sons

and if she knows how sorry I am

for not listening when she warned me

not to date the man I eventually married.

I wonder if she made the same mistake

as I when she was fifteen years younger

and I wonder if her daughter would have

faulted the same had she lived to fifteen,

and I wonder if we all make the same

mistakes over and again.

Highway 25

I remember that night we parked at the drive-in on Highway 25 and steamed up the windows before static on the AM station switched over to previews. Previews came before a raunchy, college-age comedy, alternating between rain drop rivers and lip-locked intermissions that cut through windshield fog. Foggy windows were swiped by my gray cotton jacket through your steady hand. The hand that sat on my knee during a panic attack on the drive back. The drive through dark and rain and a flooded road too immersed for good traction on those too-old tires. Tires that skidded across water when you asked if I was okay, and I just nodded my head. The head that bowed under the awning to get inside, when we stripped each other of soaked clothing, and I straddled your lap with my legs. We took laps around our troubles—the anniversary of your mom's death passing quietly with brute force, the burdens of raising two boys alone, and my cycles of manic depression—and I told you I loved you and I was sorry it was a tough night, tough year. Tough tears you'd deny, when your eyes welled up and so did mine, and we had the best sex we'd ever had on that couch while the rain just poured and poured. Words poured through your salt and pepper beard piercing my paper skin, leaving red welts I wish I could have peeled off and saved for now, when I wonder if you still make the drive to work down Highway 25 or if you finally gave them the middle finger and found something better. Found someone better.

actias luna

maybe if I whisper my love

ever so *gently*

to the words I never say

they will feel safe enough to build

a cocoon and transform

into a silk moth the size of my hand

that will settle on the collarbone

above my heart

where it will dance and flutter

lime-green wings

until it gives birth

to all the versions of myself

I tried to pack away

A Moon Poem

No, I am not sexy like her.

I am deprived of golden locks that cascade

down my back or a cat eye

sharp as steel. There is no glitter

lining the corners of my tired eyes

or red lipstick painted with precision.

I'm sexy in the way I move,

like the moon in orbit with the sun,

a force strong and unwavering, certain.

I am sexy in the way I cut your jokes in half

and serve them back to you, like a comedian

that singles out a member of the audience

under shaded eyes and asks where

your hometown resides and who you love,

but it's not me, it's her, the one

with lustrous hair and youthful lips, but oh

how tiresome it must be to always

tug her back into your orbit.

Roots Of Our Marrow

take my hand and take a seat. lose your shoes
and loosen your jaw. here, have a drink—

let the whiskey warm your throat. you should know
tomorrow will be what it is but tonight, we will make it

ours. when hills to die on outnumber mountain summits
to explore, I will take your hand and lead you through

the junipers, to a clearing filled with trillium and aster
wildflowers, where we will set our eyes upon the stars

and dream of a time to come when the roots of our marrow
will have more pull than a world engulfed by flames.

It Is May And I Am Still Waiting

Don't get married or you'll be dragging their shit around with you forever. The man with a dresser thrown over his shoulder—or was it a side table? A bedside table? Yes. It was a bedside table the man had thrown over his shoulder. It was dusk, the time of night it gets more difficult to see the blades of grass and leaves on the trees. The man cursed as he crossed the grassy median within the track and a woman's voice carried through the trees. He yelled back at her and nodded at me the way a man shakes his head as he gives his wife his credit card in a department store at Christmastime. The trees were dark, buckling under the wind. No rain, even though the meteorologist was certain we would face storms of monsoon proportions. It is May and I am still waiting for the flowers. It is May and it is dusk, and I cannot see the leaves on the trees for the darkness in the sky. The Georgia clay in this South Carolina town glows orange and I cannot tell if it is reflecting the last moments of the sunset or the glow of the streetlights that illuminate the way back home. What is home if not a person? There is no person here. There is a figure of leaves up ahead. I see his head bob

into place—leaves from the branch of one tree
bobbing above the perfect torso of another.
The one real moment in this world is born from
imitation.

Last Night Mom and Dad Bought Dinner From The Local Mexican Restaurant

and we sat at the table and talked for hours until my daughter, heavy with boredom, drifted to the living room and fell asleep on their couch. My parents talked about the burial plots they finally visited, the ones given to them years ago when we were kids, talked about my cousin who verbally and emotionally abuses my aunt and niece, how they couldn't tell her the outside cat died, how my aunt brought it to my dad in two trash bags tied up tight and how he buried it in the backyard. How my brother-in-law helped my dad board up the window and back door of the barn for the appraisal to be done for the refinance of my childhood home, the one they've lived in for thirty years, the one my mom said they would only live in for a couple of years, thirty years prior. How my niece will be four years old soon, *But Christmas is so far away!* said my mother, and we all laughed, because we knew we would blink and the tree would arrive and we would all grow older, still. We talked about my brother, how he was the only one who got out, living on an island on the Gulf side of Florida, married nine years next month, and we talked about work, all three of us, and my dad referred to himself as a *glorified construction worker*, the first time I ever heard him speak of his former career as less than proud, how the largest nuclear facility in Europe was on fire but not damaged, *Thank goodness*, because what would happen if it were? *I don't want to talk about Ukraine*, Dad said, *but Finland is scared and what if Russia decides to take Finland? What if China takes Taiwan?* and my dad said gravely, *If it ever gets that bad, you and Rylee come here and we board up the place*. When they die they want their ashes buried—they already bought a headstone. *The neighbors are the Harrises. They're super quiet*, they said, and we laughed. Mom talked about maybe buying a sitting bench close by. *There's a nice tree, too!* And Dad mentioned you can turn ashes into jewelry, into diamonds, into a tree to plant and say hello to every morning, and we laughed so hard we cried. By the time 10 o'clock approached I could feel the exhaustion in my eyes, the echoes of voices in the yellow kitchen light fog, as if I were an echo of my daughter on the couch, asleep, in the next room over, and Dad asked if they guarded us too much from the world, if they painted too positive a picture, taught us to be too trusting, and he disclosed that shattered assumptions make up a specific percentage of therapy patients who are adolescents, that adults are forgotten, never mentioned, and I see his eyes moisten. I tell him they presented the world in a hopeful light, and they did the very best with what they had, that I worry I cast too negative a light for their granddaughter, but we do the best we can. We hope our kids can see it, too, and in the end, isn't that all we can do?

Kaleidoscope

tell me again,

how many times

have I broken your heart?

you make it known so loudly.

noise bursts

from your mouth,

into the air,

& envelopes me until

I am a constant reminder

of my faults.

even I am not distracted

by your lack of question.

never once did you ask

if mine was still whole.

Just Enough

I cannot thrive on my own, as much

as I thought I could.

I killed the succulent.

The stem snapped right in half.

Watered it too much. Not enough.

Note *enough*.

All I need is a drop.

The plant cannot provide rain for itself.

Chandelier Made Of Spoons

I was browsing in that little bookstore, the one with the chandelier made of spoons, across from the restaurant with the grilled salmon salad you like when I picked up that book of poetry before I wondered if I could ever write something like that myself. The song that played overhead reminded me of the sweet scent on your collar, specific to hands that knead bread dough in a bakery, when you embraced me in the middle of that crowded downtown sidewalk. I longed to ask the cashier if she knew the song and tried desperately to remember a string of the words to look up later, but the melody charmed me into a stupor that transported me to autumn leaves and cobblestones and my gray jacket and sapphire scarf wrapped round my neck, like your arm hugged round my waist, so when I walked up to the counter to ask the cashier about the song, it had already passed. So, instead, I asked about the necklaces that hung on display made of repurposed antique keys, and I wondered if one might unlock a door to distant memories so that I could meet you on that crowded sidewalk and feel your hands warming my neck while our breath warmed the air, but I am pulled back to reality when the cashier mentions each one is handmade by a local artist, and I am reminded that you carved permanent grooves into my heart and I wonder if you ever realized that you are an artist yourself.

Eternity

if my final hallelujah is a whisper
releasing the collective prayers made
in silence at the end of my worst days,
please, tell me:
tell me it will be enough.

I know I Am Unwell When I Wander Aimlessly Around the Dollar General On A Saturday Night

and notice the dusty air vent in the ceiling. The floor feels slanted, off-kilter. I move my wallet from under my arm to my back pocket for balance, grab blueberry donuts from the shelf. They remind me of the donut holes we used to buy, a fifty count from Dunkin Donuts, the pink countertops in the house I bought when I was nineteen (always tell them you were nineteen because this will impress them, lead them to believe this college dropout had promise), and we took that picture with the sofa I found at the furniture warehouse next to the hardware store. Remember, I thought I was fat, that blue t-shirt, your shaggy auburn hair, my distorted smile recorded through the camera. The heaviness in that house, in my heart, in your hand after you punched a hole in our bedroom wall. Maybe I deserved it (I did, deserve it). White dust fell to the carpet, and the vacuum never quite sucked it all away. The edges of the air vent in the ceiling are the color of rust. The color of the coffee can on the shelf reminds me. My arms are heavy with these things, the donuts, the coffee, this grief. The card reader shuts down twice at checkout. The clerk shakes her head, says it's not my fault. Tells me this happens three times a day. I tell her it's okay, I shut down three times a day too (only three?). And we laugh.

When That Final Day Comes

might I return to the earth as a daisy

brief and full of light

or as a jellyfish

graceful and free

might I become a waterfall

certain and whole

might I return as a star

one blazing flash across the dark sky

so that you might look up and smile

<u>Hot Mustard</u>

I check the date on the now-expired milk.

The small rectangle in the refrigerator door

where most people keep butter

is where I keep spicy mustard in little packets

from the Chinese place down the road.

I think about how hot mustard

was one of few things that were mine.

I learned to love the things you did not,

including myself. Now I keep every packet

shoved into the same cubby in the fridge.

They fall like confetti each time I open the door.

I Did Ten Minutes and Twenty-One Seconds On The Exercise Bike

because a woman on Pinterest says it's how she stays motivated.

Tells herself she must do ten minutes. If she wants to quit after that, she can.

I found out that parmesan and olive oil baked a little too long

on the cookie sheet tastes like scraps of bacon.

Twenty-one seconds are lavish.

There are dishes to do, clothes to wash, but life always goes on.

I am watching one of those heartfelt shows with conflict that resolves at the end.

Twenty-one seconds is all it takes for resolution.

I've counted.

I scrape the rest of the parmesan bits into the trash can with one careful swoop.

They say freedom is of the mind. The space between your ears.

I say there is too much space between years, but seconds measured are the same.

I do. *I'm done*. Both take the same amount of time to say.

Maybe silence is golden hour minus the glow.

Take the sigh out of silence, relax the tongue, and the first syllable of my name remains.

That's right, say it.

And as the sound falls from your mouth, ask yourself why I'm not there.

If lonely tastes the same as I do.

You can quit if you want.

I am here. Seconds away.

The Thing That Terrifies Me Most

is the thought

that maybe

I have no place—

no home.

If not here,

if not heaven,

where will I go?

Where do I go

from here?

What is More Beautiful Than This

You dare me to move but I have already tried and failed

so many times that I am scared I will have to explain

this to my daughter. That this pain, this moment, is real

and sometimes we stand as tall as we can, still bent,

reaching towards a light we are not quite convinced is there.

That who we are right now is deserving of love.

That the striving is meaningless. In whatever you do,

may it be for love. To run from yourself is to run

from the beginning. There is no other place for you

than your own heart. Where else is there to go?

I am right here. So go, live your life. Give this world

all you have. It will hurt, yes—I am sorry for that.

But to feel, to feel so deeply, is to know the world.

Acknowledgments

I would like to thank the editors of the following journals in which the following poems, or versions of, were originally published:

Anti-Heroin Chic: "Honey for Houseflies"

Door Is A Jar: "Psychedelia," and *"actias luna"*

Feline Utopia Anthology: "Taking Out the Garbage on a Sunday Night"

Janus Literary: "After Picking You Up From the House I Grew Up In," and "It is May And I Am Still Waiting"

Moonstone Press Featured Poets Anthology 2021: "A Poem for Our Future"

Pages Penned in Pandemic: "Roots of Our Marrow"

Paragraph Planet: "Nights Like This"

Pithead Chapel: "Chandelier Made of Spoons"

Red Fez: "Stillness of a Songbird," and "Purple Wisteria"

Rejection Letters: "What Am I Waiting For?"

Roi Fainéant Press: "There is a Penny Under My Tongue"

Skyway Journal: "A Mercy of Good Things," "Mania," and "the boys"

Sledgehammer Lit: "When In Crisis, I Drive To the Dollar General In Search For Something," and "I Know I Am Unwell When I Wander Aimlessly Around the Dollar General On a Saturday Night"

The Cabinet of Heed: "Stream of Madness"

The Scriblerus: "Agree to Disagree"

Trampset: "The Night I met God in the drugstore"

X-R-A-Y Lit Mag: "Highway 25"

A special thank you to Between Shadows Press for publishing the following poems originally in the printing of my first chapbook, GOLDEN HOUR MINUS THE GLOW (2021):

"Untethered," "Hot Mustard," "Be Free, Little Bird," "Saturn," "The Night I Met God in the Drugstore," "Mania," "I Did Ten Minutes and Twenty-One Seconds on the Exercise Bike," "Honey for Houseflies," "Just Enough," "An Egg or Two," and "What am I waiting for?"

Thank you Claire Taylor, for offering her edits and valuable insight, and to Fred Shrum, for his support and encouragement, without whom this book would not exist.

About the Author

Lindsey is a Pushcart and Best of the Net nominated poet and writer. Her work can be found in various print and online literary journals. She is the author of poetry chapbook GOLDEN HOUR MINUS THE GLOW (Between Shadows Press, 2021). Lindsey works as an inpatient psychiatric pharmacy technician and lives with her daughter in South Carolina.

Twitter: @rydanmardsey

www.lindseyheatherly.com

www.ingramcontent.com/pod-product-compliance
Lightning Source LLC
Chambersburg PA
CBHW071246070526
44583CB00017B/2351